The Blueprints to Become Rich

Michael Frempong

||| Clink Street

London | New York

Published by Clink Street Publishing 2020

ISBN:
978-1-913568-08-5 - paperback
978-1-913568-09-2 - ebook

This book is dedicated to my mum,
Miss Georgina Mensah

Preface

Do you want to be financially free? Then you need to follow this step by step guide to enable you achieve your financial freedom. Be aware that this will involve commitment and self-discipline.

Financial Freedom could be achieved when one becomes aware of the concept of money and what to do, that is; save, invest to multiply your money.

This book outlines what you need to do to become rich, it also gives you what needs to be done at every stage in the way with practical examples. It suggests different tried and tested strategies which could be useful as you journey through the path of becoming rich. Apart from the practical examples and tried and tested strategies, useful books written by millionaires and entrepreneurs have been recommended to enable you explore more as you work your way out of poverty to a prosperous future.

Stories and parables about planning and wealth creation in the Bible as well as Bible verses relevant to how to plan, invest and make money have also been used to illustrate how to become rich.

How to get out of debt and invest for the future might be difficult because, it involves lots of sacrifices and change of habits, but I believe that if you are open, willing to change and follow the strategies and step by step guide outlined in this book, you will definitely make it and achieve your dream of becoming financially free.

Chapter 1

Planning for success

Planning is the process of thinking about and organising the programs or activities required to achieve a desired goal. It involves the creation and maintenance of a plan; it also involves preparing a sequence of events to achieve a specific goal (Wikipedia).

Planning therefore involves a sequence of events over a period to achieve a desired objective. The sequence of events or actions to achieve a desired goal should be measurable, achievable and specific with time line. If you do it effectively, you will be ready for unexpected circumstances that could affect you financially. With planning, you can reduce stress, achieve more with little effort, moreover, you will always be ahead of time.

"Planning is usually interpreted as a process to develop a strategy to achieve desired objectives, to solve problems, and to facilitate action." (Mitchell 2002).

Planning one's finances or financial planning is the process of thinking about, organising specific activities or action plans to achieve an expected goal or results.

It involves a thought process which is documented with specific action plans to achieve goals set. Planning therefore requires self-discipline and willingness to achieve targets set.

Most financial crises experienced by individuals, couples and institutions are because of no planning or poor planning.

Poor planning is better than no planning. If there is no plan, it means there are no targets set, which means that any unexpected results, whether good or bad, could be achieved. In most cases it ends up in disaster.

Most successful businessmen and rich people achieve their successes through effective planning and implementation of their action plans. It is unfortunate that I did not know the importance of planning, neither was I taught how to plan. Regrettably I didn't read, listen or watch videos to help me plan for success at the early stages of my life when I was young, however, it is better late than never. Am I now aware of the importance of planning? The answer is absolutely Yes. Thank God l have had the opportunity to listen to audio tapes, watch videos, attend workshops and read books about successful business men, millionaires, billionaires and men of God on planning. This has changed my way of thinking and have decided to share my experience with the next generation.

There are so many books written about planning – the Bible is no exception, what does the Bible teach about planning? In Genesis 41, Joseph, was called from prison to interpret Pharaoh's dreams. His interpretation of what God revealed through these dreams was so convincing that Pharaoh put him in charge of Egypt. According to the Bible, Joseph had excellent plan, he organised the storage of all surplus grain during the seven years of good harvests. He asked that one fifth of each year's harvest should be required from farmers and stored on behalf of the government. The grain was therefore stored in warehouses in nearby cities. In other words, Joseph planned to save, and the results of the effective planning and savings were amazing. This point is worth noting for further discussion on savings in Chapter 6. One can only save for a successful future if he or she plans effectively.

At the beginning of the drought, the warehouses were opened and people in Egypt could buy grain. As the situation got worse, people from neighbouring countries were allowed to buy grain too (Genesis 42:1–5).

It is important to note that effective planning will not only benefit the person who planned effectively, it has a ripple down effect on others as well. It doesn't only benefit the person in question, it can also benefit the spouse, friends and family, the community and the nation at large. This is evident in what happened to cities around Egypt because of proper and effective planning by Joseph. Joseph was guided by God, so he was able to plan carefully, and to predict what was likely to happen. Because of this, the local leadership accepted and trusted his plans. Seeking God's guidance and counsel from experts is necessary if you want your plans to be successful. Above all, present your thoughts and action plans to the almighty God and surely your plans will materialise. According to Proverbs you should *"Commit to the Lord whatever you do, and he will establish your plans."* (Proverbs 16:23)

Apart from Joseph's story in the Bible, which demonstrates effective planning, the Bible also talks about creatures that plan in good weather to be used in bad or unfavourable weather. *"Ants are creatures of little strength, yet they store up their food in the summer."* (Proverbs 30:25). Planning is therefore the most important step to take if you want to be successful or if you want to become rich. No matter the situation or circumstances one finds himself or herself in, getting out of financial crisis or stepping into the path of becoming rich begins with effective planning.

"Most plans fail, are not materialised or are not implemented because of lack of counsel, but with many advisers they succeed." (Proverbs 15:22).It is against this background that we all need to seek professional or expert advice when planning. Alternatively, you can read more, watch videos and attend seminars on planning. This will help you plan and plan effectively.

The question is how do you plan? There are six steps one could follow to plan for financial freedom.

Step 1 – Determine your current financial situation

Step 2 – Create a personal financial statement or budget

Step 3 – Set your financial goals

Step 4 – Identify alternative courses of action

Step 5 – Create and implement a financial action plan

Step 6 – Regularly review and adjust your financial plan

Determining your current financial situation involves identifying your income and expenditure and finding out whether you are spending more or less than what you are earning. This include studying your bank statement to determine money coming in and your outgoings each month.

This will enable you to create a budget by writing down all your income, expenditure and identifying any surplus or shortfall.

You can use the proforma below as a guide to create a simple financial statement to enable you assess your financial situation and develop action plans which can lead you to financial freedom.

If you have surplus or disposable income, then you are ready to invest, if you have a shortfall, then you need to reduce your expenditures or increase your income through several passive income opportunities I will be discussing later in this book, to enable you have disposable income to invest.

Having determined your financial situation and created a comprehensive budget, the next step is to set your financial goals. You need to know what you want to achieve, when you want to achieve them and how. For example, reducing your debts by 50% in the next eight months, investing £5000 in the next two years, increasing your income by £500 through passive income every month, etc.

Ensure that you set yourself a specific, measurable and achievable goals to enable you achieve your primary objectives. Setting a specific financial goal means that your goals should be clear and emphatic on what you want to achieve. Your goals should not be ambitious, however, it should be challenging. You should ensure that your goals are measurable so that you can assess whether they have been achieved or not.

The goals you would set yourself shouldn't be vague, for example, "I want to be rich soon." It would be difficult to measure this target, in addition, your goals should be achievable with specific time line to enable you determine at the end of that time frame whether those goals have been achieved or not. You therefore need to think about your goals carefully before setting them, two or three goals at a time should be ok.

The question is what do you want to achieve? If you want to be rich in ten or twenty years from now, what could you do to achieve this? Do you want to invest £100 a month for the next twenty years? Do you want to buy ten houses in the next ten years? Ensure that all these goals are documented with specific action plans to achieve them.

Alternative courses of action should be put in place to ensure that your plans are not disrupted. Measures should be put in place to avoid unnecessary external pressures to destroy a well thought out plan. It is therefore advisable to evaluate alternatives thoroughly. Think about the pros and cons of the alternatives, what can be done differently to achieve the same goals, adjustments to be made and at what cost. Moreover, who would be affected either positively or negatively.

The most important part of the planning process is to create and implement an action plan. This involves working out your income and coming up with other ways of increasing your income. It also involves reducing your expenditures and sticking to the monthly budget you have planned with the personal financial statement. This aspect of the planning process requires self-discipline and willingness to sacrifice. This could mean cutting down on some activities, habits, or even changing your lifestyle. Since human beings don't want change, most excellent plans are thrown out of gear when it comes to implementing the action plans. You need to think carefully and establish whether you are prepared to sacrifice now and become financially free or rich and enjoy the lifestyle you want after that, or you want to remain in your current situation and run your finances like a train being controlled by remote control without any specific destination in mind. Most people don't plan their finances and this leads to the accumulation of debts which subsequently causes domestic problems, depression and even suicide.

It is imperative to note that planning enables you to manage your life better and prevent unnecessary stress and depression, which can also lead to heart diseases and some form of cancers. Effective planning should therefore bring about excitement for a brighter future ahead not sorrow and anguish. Knowing that you could be debt free or acquire a certain number of assets, or you could stop working and be your own boss, by relying on your passive income in the near future as a result of prudent planning of your finances, should indeed be exciting and refreshing.

Changes in circumstances could affect your plan either positively or negatively – because of this, you should regularly review and adjust your financial plan if necessary to suit your personal needs.

Before reading the next chapter, ensure that you have completed your personal financial statement with rough estimate using a pencil, and cross check it with your bank statement later. You could complete this statement individually, with your partner, or as a couple.

Personal Financial Statement

Income	£	Expenditure	£
Wages		Rent or Mortgage	
Passive income		Gas and Electricity	
Jobseeker's Allowance		Council tax/ Water Bill	
Employment Support Allowance		Phone (Landline and Mobile)	
Income Support		TV (Licence + Satellite/Cable)	
Tax Credits		Home and Life Insurance	
Child Benefit		Food	
Incapacity Benefit		Childcare	
Disability Living Allowance		Credit Card Payment	
Housing Benefit		Loan payment	
Carer's Allowance		Debt Collector Payment	
Child Maintenance		Public transport/Petrol	
Any other Benefits		Car insurance/ tax/MOT	
		Entertainment/ Clothing	
		Subscription	
		Other expenses	
TOTAL income		**TOTAL expenditure**	
Budget deficit/ Disposable income			

Chapter 2

What you need to invest first

Most people who have the money to invest often do not know what to invest in or how to invest. Others are of the view that they don't have money or enough money to invest after paying all bills, so wouldn't even think of investing.

Investment is not just about money, you can either invest in your time, your money and most importantly your own self. These types of investments would indirectly lead to financial freedom.

If you want to be rich, the first thing you need to do is to invest in yourself. This involves; reading books about wealth creation, attending seminars or workshops, watching YouTube videos about successful businessmen and entrepreneurs, etc.

I recommend you invest more time reading books on planning, management and how to establish your own business. These books changed my way of thinking and motivated me to start planning for my future. Reading these books challenged me to think outside the box and explore more about wealth creation and how to manage my finances. You can watch YouTube videos about how to become rich and other related videos about wealth creation. I have been dedicating two hours a day to watch videos about how to be financially free. I have also been listening to audio tapes of books including the one written by Warren Buffets, Benjamin Graham and many others.

Wealth creation books written by these rich authors are a good read as you prepare to invest in yourself.

One person who inspired me the most is Dr Myles Munroe, may his gentle soul rest in perfect peace. Listening to Dr Myles's audio tapes and watching videos of his sermons have been a blessing to me and have re-energised my quest to invest in myself.

According to one of his sermons, God has planted in every human being a talent, and this talent has the potential for making everybody a millionaire. The main task which is also the most important thing is to identify your gift or talent and pursue it. According to Dr Myles, the wealthiest places on Earth is the cemetery, because, most of the gifts or talents that could have made millions but couldn't be harnessed have been buried in the cemetery. So, identifying your talent is the key to become rich. He stated in one of his sermons which is also outlined in one of the numerous books he has written, that 9am–5pm should be dedicated to your job, however, 5pm–midnight should be set aside for your own private business or self-development. He quoted Ecclesiastes 11:6 which states "Sow your seed in the morning, and at evening let your hands not be idle, for you do not know which will succeed, whether this or that, or whether both will do equally well." It is evident in this Bible verse that investing in yourself in the evening could potentially provide a passive income opportunity which could supplement your main job and eventually enable you to save to invest leading to your financial freedom.

It is important to note that you can become rich if you have a source of decent income and then with prudent planning and management of your resources, invest and watch your money 'grow'.

If you are in a gainful employment, you should treat your job with the outmost importance and work diligently to improve the organisation and the sector you are working for. In addition, you must make yourself relevant and needed in such a way that when you leave your job, your absence would be felt. Furthermore, you should make yourself irreplaceable, however, you should train your subordinates or people around you to be able to fill your position when you are not there, this is a sign of a good leader .To be able to do this, you must invest in yourself first, you should use every opportunity and resource available to you in your current employment to learn new things, develop your skills and train yourself. Your employers have the moral if not legal duty to train you to do your job effectively; capitalise on this opportunity and train yourself while you are still working for your employer. Investing in yourself to enable you carry out your current job effectively and improving yourself for your future career is non-negotiable, so you should improve your skills for your role in your current employment. Attend management and leadership courses for promotion, improve your IT skills by attending IT training or enrolling on a course in IT to keep abreast with the fast-growing technology. Teachers for example, could read more about the new specifications, watch videos of outstanding lessons on YouTube and teachers TV, read about the new education policies and programs amongst others.

Spending your spare time meaningfully to develop your skills or work towards becoming rich is crucial. This could be a small business you are running, books you are reading, a course you have enrolled in, books you are writing, blog on Facebook you are working on, live YouTube videos you are doing etc.

Identifying your talent or gift would enable you to focus more on what skills you need to spend your time to develop. Once you are able to identify your talent, you need to harness it in your own 'working time', i.e. 5pm–midnight.

Invest in yourself by attending business seminars on how to establish a business, how to invest in stocks or properties, trade in forex, how to start online business or shop.

I had an amount of money I wanted to invest for higher returns, however, I didn't know how to invest this money to yield a decent return. I didn't want to invest in an ISA because the interest on it is negligible, so I contacted a friend who is an accountant for an advice, but he couldn't help me on what to do. I went to my bank for professional advice, guess what? It was a wasted journey. I became frustrated and thought about investing in Treasury bills or bonds in Ghana where I originally come from, so I did my research and realised that I could double the money I was looking to invest in five years. However, I was concerned about rate of inflation which could affect the exchange rate and potentially reduce the profit margin. Even though I overcame these fears after thorough research, I wanted to go to Ghana to invest this money personally. While I was waiting for the right time to travel to Ghana, unexpected and unplanned family commitments cropped up which wiped out almost all the money leaving me with only a fraction of it. I became worried that I couldn't invest this money for better returns as I originally planned and had virtually wasted it. I then decided to invest in myself by watching YouTube videos, reading books, attending training sessions, workshops and researching on the internet about investment ideas. I eventually decided to buy shares in the stock market. I therefore researched extensively and came across a platform I could use to invest in shares. This platform was recommended by Money Expert. Money Expert is one of the UK's leading comparison sites, which provides useful information for customers to enable them get the best deals on a wide range of products. I had earlier on spent two hours a day watching videos for almost a month and had also been reading extensively on how to invest in shares for beginners, I therefore invested at least twenty hours just watching different videos to educate myself on stocks, bonds, what to invest and also how to invest among others. These videos then led me to read useful books like *The Intelligent Investor* by Benjamin Graham. Because of this education, I became confident and ready to execute my first investment in shares. I got excited after knowing the key things to look for before investing in shares. I invested in shares which had high dividend yield and had good prospects according to their financial report. Again, I had to spend most evenings from 5–10pm reading financial reports of different companies before investing. I followed the advice of other experience brokers and what Benjamin Graham suggested in his book to make my first investment.

Later on, I attended seminars and workshops on how to trade in the stock market to enable me trade in the stock market as well.

Other investment opportunities will be dealt with in the subsequent chapters.

Now jot down three things you want to do in order to invest in yourself before reading the next chapter, for example; watch YouTube videos, read books, research on the internet, etc.

Chapter 3

Exploring the financial group you belong to

Having a good financial plan is like having a vehicle ready for a journey. It is essential to make provisions for funds available to fuel the vehicle ready to embark on the journey. Lack of fuel will affect the journey unless alternative arrangements are made to make the journey. It will be difficult to execute an excellent plan if you are not in a gainful employment or have no source of income. People in some developed countries are normally supported financially if they lose their jobs or are not able to work due to health problems. Because of the opportunities available in these countries, people living in such countries including UK who are not in gainful employment also have the opportunity to become rich through prudent management of the funds they receive from the government. If you are not fortunate to be living in such countries, then you should aim at getting a job that can bring decent income every month, otherwise, it will be difficult to achieve your dream of becoming rich unless you win a lottery, which is not what I will advise you to do if you want to become rich. The only solution is to invest in yourself and take it from there. If you are in a gainful employment, you could invest in yourself to improve your skills to enable you get promotion at your current employment and get pay rise. In addition to improving your skills and constantly working towards getting a pay increase, you should also think about using your own "working hours", 5pm–midnight to improve your own talents or do something that can earn you passive income.

There are certain questions you should be asking yourself constantly and work towards finding answers to them. Take a moment and answer the following questions:

Have you identified your God-given talent(s)?

Are you still working towards developing yourself to ensure that you can get passive income from your own investments?

Have you begun to see the fruits of your investments?

If the answer to any of these questions is no, don't worry, all you need to do is to start working towards getting answers to these questions.

In my view, young people are in a better position than their older counterparts because, they have the opportunity to start from a clean sheet and also know what to do early enough to have a significant impact in their finances over time. They also have enough time on their hands to make their millions while young and enjoy the fruits of their labour.

People can be categorised into different groups based on their financial status. The groupings are so fluid and volatile that you can move from one group to another easily. Moving from one group to another could be as a result of losing your job, becoming bankrupt or becoming financially literate and managing your finances well.

The total amount of money people receive as their income at the end of the month can be used to categorise them into four main groups.

The first category of people who belong to Group 1 are those whose main source or sources of income are financial support from the government, this could be: Disability Living Allowance, Income Support, Incapacity Benefit, Jobseeker's Allowance, etc. This is only applicable to countries like UK, Germany, etc. whose governments support their citizens financially if they are not able to work or are working but not earning enough money.

The amount of money people in this group get might not be enough, however, some of them also get other benefits such as Tax Credit, Housing Benefit, Council Tax Support in addition to the income support they receive. The total amount of money they receive each month is almost the same as the amount of money some of the people who are in gainful employment are earning. In view of this, if the money people in this group receive is managed well, some could be saved to invest.

The second category of people belong to Group 2; in my view, this group has the highest number of people. This category of people consists of the main workforce and the backbone of every country. They are mostly the employees in our society, this includes the public-sector workers such as Nurses, Teachers, Social workers, Clerks, Secretaries, factory workers, labourers, cleaners among others.

Unfortunately, most of the people in Group 1 and 2 are either poor, feed from hand to mouth, or only work to pay bills and debts. There are many people who are not able to cope with the pressure from their creditors especially when reminder letters or threatening letters begin to come through the letter box; as a result of this, some people become stressed or depressed because of debts. There are few reported cases where people have committed suicide because of debts. It is also generally believed and scientifically proven that some of the health conditions are linked to stress and depression.

Most people in Group 1 and 2 have what they need in life to be happy and therefore are OK with what they have, so long as they can have a roof over their head or pay their mortgage and afford their holidays every year.

Most of the people who belong to Group 2 are public sector workers as discussed earlier. They work to keep the public services running smoothly. These group of people work hard, however, they earn less money because government take substantial amount of money from them as taxes to build schools, roads, hospitals, etc. In the developed countries, the taxes the government deducts from these people, together with other taxes collected, are normally put to good use to improve the lives of their citizens, in the developing countries, not all the taxes collected from this category of people are put to good use. The money is virtually divided into three, two-thirds goes into the pockets of corrupt politicians and some public sector workers, it is only one-third that is used to develop the country, even with that, the price of the projects are highly inflated in such a way that only half of that amount is used in developing the country. Whereas people in Group 2 work hard and get little for their money, it's the direct opposite when you move up the group.

The next category of people who belong to Group 3 are normally self-employed, these are mostly small-scale business owners who employ a few people, They tend to get tax breaks or there is a flexible tax system to help them expand their businesses and employ more people. Since private sector is said to be an engine of growth in most countries, empowering the private sector will enable them to create more jobs because government alone cannot create jobs for everyone in the country.

Highly skilled professionals, Doctors, Bankers, Lawyers, Accountants, Heads of institutions, CEOs, etc. are also categorised into Group 3. Most of the people in this category are financially sound because they earn good income. People in this category are able to save enough money to invest. With financial education, good planning and prudent management of their finances, they can easily become rich. An economic downturn or recession could affect some of the people in this category. People in this category could therefore move to Group 2 or even Group 1 due to circumstances, sometimes beyond their control. If small scale business owners are not able to manage their business well and lose their businesses, they could also move to Group 1 or Group 2.

It is worth noting that establishing a business is the easiest way of becoming rich, all it takes is a business idea. An idea in my view is simply wealth. Having an idea that can solve a problem can easily make you rich. This is the main reason why people who have business ideas and are able to set up their own business make it big. You could easily move to Group 3 if you can develop an idea which has the potential of solving a problem. Most of the small and big business owners and the richest people in the world have reached where they are because they had an idea, developed it and made them work. If you have an idea or business plan that can solve a problem, invest in yourself, seek professional advice and support from experts, above all, commit your time and energy to it, you will be on your way to become rich. There are so many business ideas you can look into, you can also research more on business ideas and how to set up your own business to enable you move to Group 3.

The fourth group of people belong to Group 4, These are the big business owners and Investors. These are the richest people in our communities. According to a Credit Suisse report, as of 2017 only one percent of the world's population was wealthy and the wealthiest owned more than half of the world's wealth.

The percentage of the richest people in our community is very small. The question is, why are some people very rich and others very poor? The answers I believe could be endless, however, there is basic principle of money which can either make you rich or poor. The basic principle is whether you spend and borrow or save and invest. The rich people and those in Group 4 tend to save and invest or lend whereas the poor people spend and borrow. In order to move to Group 3 and 4, one needs to start saving and investing. No amount is too small to invest, All you need to do is find the right investment opportunity for you to start.

It important to note that those in Groups 3 and 4 normally pay themselves first and deduct all their expenses before paying tax on what is left, whereas those in Group 2 and some people in Group 3 have their taxes deducted from their pay first and what is left is given to them as their salary from which all expenses would be deducted. You can only save and invest what is available after tax and expenses.

There are few books out there on how the rich or business people pay less tax, research more on it if you want to know more about the unfairness in the tax system. Even though this is not the topic for discussion, it is important to be aware of this loophole or unfairness in the tax system so that you can plan your way out of Group 2.

Few people from Group 3 happen to migrate to the next group, Group 4 by chance or due to prudent financial management. My main aim is to outline the blueprints needed to move to a higher group for people in Groups 1 and 2 to enable them move to Group 3 and eventually to Group 4. It will not be easy, neither will it happen overnight but I strongly believe that this blueprints or step by step guides, are what one need to be able to make it to Group 3 or group 4.

The question one might ask when reading this book is "How do I become rich if I don't work?" The Bible even states that he who do not work should not eat.

"For even when we were with you, we gave you this rule: 'The one who is unwilling to work shall not eat.'" (2 Thessalonians 3:10).

You don't need to be employed to work, all you need to do is to identify your talent and harness it. Even if you can't go out and take up 9–5pm job, there are so many things you can do at home to earn money. Working from home has become very popular because of improved technology in our society and the easy access to the internet. Most people do all their shopping online, some local councils or boroughs have made provisions for their employees to work from home, moreover, social media has also presented a huge opportunity to make money in the comfort of your home in your spare time. This ranges from setting up an online store to making videos on the YouTube. Of late you can make videos on the YouTube to make money, start online business or even write books to earn you an income. This could be your main source of income or serve as passive income.

Chapter 4

Starting from a clean sheet

People who don't have any debts or have just started their first employment, especially our young people, should count themselves lucky to be reading this book now and should avoid spending more money than they earn. Spending more that you earn is the cause of debt accumulation, which eventually leads to financial crisis for most people. Avoid using loans or credit cards to supplement your monthly household budget. They are there as a 'life support' not for daily use. If you use it then you must pay the total amount within a month to avoid paying interest on it.

If you have already locked up yourself in debts, don't worry, you need to work yourself out of these debts. Start afresh by planning how to pay off all your debts. You might either negotiate with your debtors to pay specific amount of money per month till you pay off all the debt or decide to declare yourself bankrupt and stop paying any of the debts apart from your mortgage till you become financially sound.

Whether you declare yourself bankrupt and start afresh or negotiate with your creditors to pay an agreed amount you can afford according to your personal budget, the consequences are that it will affect your credit ratings and might affect your chances of getting credit in the future or you would get credit with very high interest rate.

In the UK, credit records are kept on your file for five years, after five years you can rebuild your credit from a clean sheet.

In view of this, if your loan and credit card payments exceed your income after paying your utility bills, food and transport, then it is advisable to seek professional advice on what to do. Alternatively, you can stop paying your debts if you are finding it difficult to support yourself and your family financially. You might have a poor credit rating which could affect your credit record, however, you will have the opportunity to rebuild your credit after five years to restart from the scratch.

Sometimes it is better to ignore all creditors especially loans, store cards and credit cards and focus on rebuilding your finances than to attempt to pay them, especially if you cannot genuinely afford them. If you have a loan or credit card with the same bank your salary is paid in, then you might have to open another account with another bank so that your loan is not deducted from your account before you have access to your money for bills, rent, food and transport, which are essential needs to keep you going.

If other banks wouldn't open an account for you, search for your local credit union, they operate just like banks and they will open an account for you whether you are in financial difficulties or not. This account could be given to your employer to pay your salary through so that you can have access to all your salary and plan with it. It is advisable to pay off your debts and start from a clean sheet if you can afford to pay them.

Being in debt or in a financial crisis can be daunting, however, it is important to treat every problem in your life as a challenge and realise that every challenge comes with an opportunity. It is of the general view that many businesses spring up during global financial crisis. In the midst of economic challenges comes an opportunity to unlock many potentials. People who lose their jobs have no option than to think outside the box and come out with a business plan and start their own business, because no one is employing and most employees are also being laid off. It is therefore essential to see the financial challenges you might be facing as an opportunity to establish a business or start something new that can earn you some passive income.

Joseph in the Bible had to go to prison for something he hadn't done, it was a huge challenge in his life, but what happened after his ordeal? He later became the second most powerful person in Egypt, the Prime Minister who eventually had to save his own family who sold him to strangers.

Below is a step by step guide on how to pay off your debt. The rule for paying off your debt is to stop borrowing or accumulating more debts. The slogan is *"If you don't have you don't spend."*

Debt repayment is crucial should you want to move into the next group as discussed earlier.

Paying debts also requires planning, you need to list all your debts, write down the amount left to be paid, the number of months left to pay and the interest rate on it. Refer to your personal budget and write down your disposable income. You need to jot down the smallest debt with the highest interest rate and pay that one first. For example, if you have credit card with an outstanding balance of £2000 with interest rate 29.9%, a loan of £5000 with interest rate of 9.9% and another loan of £10,000 with interest rate of 20%, you need to plan how to pay the credit card with interest rate of 29.9% first followed by the £10,000 before planning to pay for the £5000.

Work out how long it will take you to pay off the first debt with the disposable income, do the same calculation with the other loans. This will give you rough idea as to when you will pay off all your debts.

For example, if your disposable income is £100 a month, it means it will take you maximum of twenty months to pay off that loan. It is important not to miss payment to incur any further charges since all the debts are budgeted for in your personal monthly budget. If circumstances change, negotiate with your debtors to avoid further charges. You should look for extra sources of income to increase your disposable income to pay off the loans quicker. As soon as you get extra income through pay rise or other passive income, don't just spend it, increase your loan repayments. At this stage you should be guided by two financial statements, your personal financial statement and your debt repayments plan.

Personal Debt Repayment Plan

Creditor	What kind of debt	Balance owed	Repayment amount	Number of months to repay
			TOTAL	

Once you are determined to rebuild your finances on a clean sheet, stick to your plan and avoid extra borrowing. As discussed earlier, you have to look at your personal financial statement again and do two things;

1. Increase your earnings through passive income and
2. Reduce your outgoings through savings.

Some passive income ideas have already been discussed in the previous chapter. Find out which one will suit you; alternatively you can find another job to increase your income, start an online business or join any network marketing business that would not involve any high start-up cost.

May I share the experience of a friend who had no job when he came to London from Africa? This young man came to London thinking that life is easy, it got to a time when he had virtually no money to live on. He then decided to do anything to earn an income so he started ironing people's clothes for few pounds, this ironing business kept on growing. He identified services people needed and began to provide these services. He eventually became a handyman and therefore decided to invest in himself. He then invested in his time and learnt gardening. It will surprise you to know the number of people who are having difficulty in maintaining their own garden and therefore need gardening services. He continued providing these services and later on invested in more equipment, because, he wanted to do his work effectively. This young man has now established his own small-scale gardening and ironing business and has been earning decent amount of money to look after his family. He is now in a better position to expand this business and even employ more people. I know few people who went to college to study part time plumbing and mechanics. This is earning them extra income.

I also know a lady in London who migrated from one of the Eastern European countries whose husband was a handyman and injured his back so couldn't support his family anymore.

The income support he receives is not enough to enable him to live the lifestyle he is used to. This lady is extremely hard working and has been cleaning people's houses to earn money, when she cleans, you would fall in love with her work. She normally uses the cleaning materials in the house and often suggest the cleaning materials you should buy if the ones she needs to do her job effectively are not available. She has been doing this cleaning to support her family in this challenging times at no start-up cost.

Getting an extra income is extremely important if you want to pay off your debts or want to rebuild your finances. Learning how to plait hairs is another way of making decent income. A lady I spoke to when researching about passive income and how much it can bring to the family, told me that she earns between £800–£1000 a week. Another lady who is a seamstress quoted similar amount. All these passive income opportunities require identifying an area of interest or gifting, investing in yourself to harness this gift and making an effort to start to something straight away.

Reducing your outgoings could be challenging, however, you could sacrifice certain behaviour or way of life to rebuild your life for a better future.

Reducing your outgoings through savings can also help. It cost more to use electricity during the day time compared to night time, some energy providers also charge between 2–10p per unit cheaper than others. It is therefore advisable to shop around and use a cheaper utility provider, moreover, use electrical appliances such as washing machine, dishwasher and iron during off-peak periods instead of peak periods. Off-peak normally ranges between 6pm to 6am, therefore if you use your electricity during this time it is cheaper.

As a result of this, using electrical appliances in the evening will save you money, it might not be much, but it will add up to make a difference. Ironing could also be done in the evening instead of doing it in the morning to cost you more in your electricity bills. If you have kids, then do the ironing of their school uniforms in the evenings.

Also buy energy saving bulbs, these LED bulbs will not just save you money on the cost of energy you use, but they also last long and therefore save money replacing these bulbs every now and then.

Joining a discount club or having reward cards that enables you to save money when you shop is a good idea.

There are many discount clubs with such offers around; do your research and ensure that you are reducing your expenditures through savings as well.

Many people shop only on sales, there are many seasons and periods you can buy to save a lot of money, I had wanted to buy Smart TV from a shop, the TV had been reduced from £529 to £399, when I went to the shop two weeks later to buy, it had increased to £449, I refused to buy the TV at that price, fortunately I realised that Black Friday which is normally in November was three weeks away, when I checked on online on black Friday it had been reduced to £379; this is the price I paid for the TV.

I like TESCO's slogan 'Why pay more?' You can shop on Boxing Day and other festive occasions when shops normally reduce their prices to save more money.

Refinancing or renegotiating your loans or credit cards is another way of reducing your outgoings. Once you start building your finances, your credit will gradually improve, you will therefore be eligible for lower interest loans or credit. Study how much you owe and figure out if taking another loan at a lower interest rate would enable you pay off the high interest loan at a shorter time. You can also visit your creditors and find out if they can save you money. Some banks reward loyalty and length of time you have banked with them, visit your local branch and find out offers available.

Refinancing your credit card is another way of saving money, there could be zero percentage (0%) balance transfer offer available to you, use it to pay off the existing credit cards with high interest you are currently paying every month without reducing the actual credit amount. When you have two or three months to the end of the 0% transfer period, look for another 0% transfer deal for example twelve or twenty-four months and use it to pay your credit cards, by so doing you will be paying off your credit card without paying any interest on it. Be aware that there is always about 1% or 2% balance transfer fee which is a one-off fee to pay when doing the balance transfer. This is better than paying interest every month on the outstanding balance on the credit card. You can also use your credit card to pay for goods and services without paying any interest so long as you pay the full amount within a month. For example, if your credit card bill date is 1st of every month and the payment due date is 26th of every month, you can spend the credit card just after the bill date which is 1st of the month when the credit card statement has been generated for that month and pay the total amount on or before the payment due date which is 26th. By so doing you will be able to have access to funds for your transactions or business without paying any interest.

Chapter 5

How to raise a capital for investment

Whether you are financially sound i.e. you have decent disposable income or in financial difficulties, you need to have multiple streams of income. If the extra income you get every month is managed well, then you will be on your way of fulfilling your dreams to become rich. There are so many things people can do to earn them passive income, you can invest in yourself to train as a hair stylist, nail stylist, makeup artist, etc. to earn passive income to supplement your main source of income. Most colleges offer these courses at highly subsidised prices. You can even speak to your local hair stylist to find out if they can allow you to work voluntarily and understudy them. Try few places, in most cases they would be more than willing to have extra hand at no cost to them. This can be done in your own convenient time, maybe two evenings or weekends.

Online sales is the most popular one, you can buy clearance goods and sell them on the internet either on a website or Facebook, tag more people and advertise at no cost. You can also sell on Amazon which is a massive online market.

You can have a blog, upload videos on YouTube and encourage more people subscribe, you earn more money if you have more viewers and subscribers.

Health professionals can make videos on healthy diet, personal hygiene and any other relevant health related issues that could benefit people.

Weightlifters and people who love to exercise can make exercise videos and share them on YouTube; this will earn you money forever so long as people like the videos and view or subscribe to your YouTube channel.

You can upload more videos to help tone different parts of the body.

People in the health profession such as Nurses, Doctors and Pharmacists as well as industry workers could do overtime to earn extra income.

Those in the Teaching profession could also make videos on how to teach outstanding lesson, upload strategies on how to manage behaviour in class and many more. Depending on the number of viewers or subscribers to their YouTube channel, they could be paid. In addition, they could also make videos on how to teach specific topics and upload them. They could also do one-to-one home tuition and teach students privately, or run a home tuition centre where students are taught in the evenings or weekends by group of teachers to earn extra income.

Online videos explaining different topics have been useful to most students, even teachers sometimes use such videos in their lessons, this means there could be more viewers over a long period of time. So long as the topic remains in the school curriculum those who make such videos would earn passive income.

Teachers could sell their own PowerPoint presentations, worksheets, schemes of work and any other teaching resources they have prepared on TES for extra income.

Plumbers, Electricians, Carpenters and handymen could also make videos to teach people how to solve various problems. Such videos also have the potential of earning passive income.

A network marketing business is another way of making extra income. There are so many out there, one network marketing business encourages people to save in gold on a monthly basis, as you introduce more people to save for their own future you get commission, Some network marketing business involves selling items including toiletries, others involves selling makeup and many more things.

Just do your own research and sign up to the one you are interested in, it could even be a product you already use.

People who are talented public speakers could also work on motivational speeches and deliver them for extra income. Writing books is another way of earning extra income. Robert Kiyosaki and Dr Myles Munroe and many other authors have made millions with their books. If you have the passion to write, do so and get your book published to earn you passive income. The author of Harry Potter had the passion for writing and now worth millions.

Before reading the next chapter, write down at least two passive income ideas you would want to try to enable you earn passive income and raise capital for investment.

You could also prepare rough business plan to start your own business, for example what you intend to do, when you are going to start, what the start-up cost is, how much you intend to earn per month, who to contact for advice, etc.

If it will involve a huge capital, you need to find out how much it will cost and where you would get the money from. It is advisable to start a business or passive income idea that would require very little or no capital. For example, you can use your own phone to upload videos on your YouTube channel. All these strategies would enable you raise capital to support your personal budget and invest.

To be able to raise a capital to invest, you need to follow the fifty, thirty, ten, ten percent 50/30/10/10% principle.

This principle states that 50% of your income should go into your needs, 30% goes into your wants and the remaining 20% should go into paying debts and savings for investment.

According to this principle, 50% of your income should go towards your needs which includes housing i.e. mortgage or rent, utility bills, medical bills, fuel, transport or travel costs, etc. These are your personal needs you must settle as soon as you are paid to keep you going. Your rent or mortgage provide you with the shelter you need. If your salary or pay cheque is not capable of supporting any of the 50% items listed above and therefore pushing the percentage beyond 50%, then you need to review your personal budget or find a job that can pay you enough money to cater for these items. Alternatively, you could reduce the total amount of money that goes into your needs to make the 50%. Here are few suggestions on what to do; you can rent a smaller house or room, you can also use the bus instead of train because bus pass is relatively cheaper than travel card.

If you have a mortgage, you could rent some rooms out, if it's one-bedroom house or flat you can convert the living room to a bedroom and rent it out or vice versa. Alternatively, you can live with family and friends until you can earn enough money to support all the things you desperately need.

A renowned millionaire and a preacher, Dr Myles Munroe, in one of his popular sermons stated that he and his wife had to live with his mother-in-law for some time at the early stages of their marriage to save money to enable them to acquire their own property. Later on, in his life, he eventually acquired and lived in over a million-dollar property in an affluent area in Bahamas.

According to the 50/30/10/10% principle, you should allocate 30% of your net income on the things you want, for example clothing, holidays, buying a car, buying mobile phones or paying for mobile phone bills, leisure or entertainment such as going out for dinner, cinema, etc.

It is important to treat yourself or enjoy life once you are working. This will enable you to de-stress and relax to re-energise you to carry on working hard. The body needs a break, just like machines need MOT and servicing, treating yourself is therefore necessary.

If you want to buy a car or go for vacation, the money should come from 30% of the money you earn every month. Some people contribute to a holiday program so that they don't have to take a huge amount of money from their bank account which sometimes can be challenging. It is important that this is planned and budgeted for in your personal financial statement. Sticking to your personal budget might mean sacrificing certain things, these could involve not going on holiday every year, cutting your expenditure on clothes you buy and reducing how many times you go out for entertainment.

The other 20% should be split into two, half should be used to pay your loans, for example car loan, credit card, store card or any debt that is planned in your financial statement.

The other half should be set aside to build your investment portfolio. This amount could be deducted from your salary or you can set up a direct debit to channel the amount into a savings account possibly an ISA account or investment account. The money in this account could build up and eventually used for investment every three to four months. Some financial institutions offer a guaranteed 4% return per annum on your investments, so long as you have enough money to meet the minimum amount for investment. You can invest with such financial institutions until you are confident enough to invest in stocks yourself. You can even buy gold or silver which can appreciate in value over time or start a business. Some people especially those who are debt free donate 10% of their income to charity of their choice. Some Christians and Sikhs pay tithes and therefore contribute 10% of their income to their local church or temple to support the gospel or provide resources, items or even food for people in their community. The Bible urges all Christians to give cheerfully because there is blessing in giving than receiving. It states that "Each of you should give what you have decided in your heart to give, not reluctantly or under compulsion, for God loves a cheerful giver." (2 Corinthians 9:7).

It is important to note that the 50/30/10/10% principle is just a guide to enable you plan your finances effectively. Setting 10% of your income aside to invest is non-negotiable if you want to be rich. Unless you are paying off your debts using the debt repayment plan outlined in the previous chapter, you should make it a habit to save every month.

If you have a huge loan to pay off, then it is not advisable to invest, finish paying off the loan and then start investing. If the loan payment is manageable or already planned for, then you can use the 10% of the 50/30/10/10% principle to pay it off while investing with the other 10%.

Chapter 6

Investing for the future

Most people have opened savings account but there is no money in the account, the money that is usually saved doesn't last long in the account because of our spending habits. We always want to buy that bag, those shoes or that car. We should always set aside some amount of money that should only be saved with the intention of investing. The money should therefore be saved for a short period of time and then invest.

Saving for a short time and investing the money for a long time is the key to become rich.

There are different ways of saving, a few people save in piggy banks and invest the money yearly, others save money in an ISA account, some people team up, contribute money and give it to one person, this is rotated amongst them until all the members of that group have had their turn, by so doing each member receives a lump sum of money when it gets to their turn-this is popularly known as 'susu'.

Those who work in the public sector mostly contribute specific amount of money each month to their pension. Some people rather pay certain amount of money each month into an investment account either with a bank or other financial institutions who provide platforms for investing in shares, mutual funds, etc. Imagine you save £1 a day in a piggy bank every day at the age of 18, you will be able to save £365 every year to invest.

Would this work for most people? the answer is no, however, those who can do it could go ahead and save for investment using this method. Since there is no harm in trying, it is advisable to try at least one of the aforementioned savings method to invest for your future or any saving method that works for you.

Investing in stocks, mutual funds or trading in the stock market is one way of becoming rich. Stock represents a claim on the company's assets and earnings, it is worth noting that a share of the stock represents owning a fraction of the corporation in proportion to the total number of shares available. Investing in stocks is just like owing a fraction of a company.

There are different types of stocks, different stocks have different level of risk. The type of stock I will recommend especially for people who want to start investing or those who are beginners in investment are 'Blue-Chip' stocks. Blue-Chip stocks are stocks of the biggest companies in the country. These are usually high-quality companies with years of strong profits and steady dividend payments. They are the most safest stocks to invest in. Investing in Blue-Chip companies is like investing in the most safest companies that have been around for decades, some twenty years, fifty years, etc. Examples of Blue-Chip stocks are MacDonald's, Coca-Cola, etc. Investing in such companies over a long period of time will enable you to accumulate wealth to make you rich.

Some companies pay higher dividends than others, it is therefore necessary to do your own research to buy stocks in companies which are stable and also pay higher dividend. Dividend is the profit that is paid to investors depending on percentage they have invested or 'bought'. The dividends are either paid quarterly or yearly.

Most companies pay small percentage of the dividend to their shareholders. Some pay a relatively high percentage of the dividend whereas others don't pay dividends at all.

Normally the dividend that are paid to shareholders ranges from 1.3% to 6%. When investing in stocks it is essential that you do your research to find a Blue-chip company that pay high dividend. It is important to research more into Blue-Chip companies or companies which are stable and safe to invest. Some banks, pharmaceutical companies, oil companies and real estate developers which are safe to invest in their shares pay decent dividends ranging from 5% to 8% per annum.

Apart from the dividend or profit that is shared quarterly or yearly, the share price could also go up. This means that apart from earning profits or dividends, you could also earn extra money when you sell your shares after holding it for at least a year or two.

Stocks can be categorised based on their risk level. There are high-risk stocks, intermediate and low risk or safe stocks to invest in. High-risk stocks normally pay high dividends, the share price can fluctuate, which means you can gain a substantial amount of money if you sell when share prices are high or lose a significant amount of your investments if you sell when shares are low. This sort of stocks is left to those who are expert in trading in the stock market. Intermediate risk stocks are shares that pay between 3–5% dividends, this include shares in banks, oil companies, etc.

It is advisable to invest in the long term, for example twenty years or more; in the medium term, between five and twenty years; or in the short term between six months and five years.

Investing in shares will not give you quick money, you should therefore have patience and discipline to invest for a long term. If you invest in the right shares at the right time, you can make a significant gain. Those who invested in the Bitcoin at the price of $1 per share are now millionaires, because, one share is now selling at about $14,000 dollars.

Some companies offer shares as a token to their workers for their contribution to the company, others allow their workers to buy shares at a reasonable price. You should take advantage and buy these shares in your company provided the company is sustainable.

Reading financial reports of companies to get relevant information about them are crucial to assist you make the right decision if you want to invest in stocks.

Those who cannot find time to read these reports can still invest in mutual funds with their banks or other financial institutions; most of the investment banks and financial institutions have account managers who would do all the background work and invest the money on your behalf, however, this comes with a small fee.

Remember the first thing you need to do before investing your money is to invest in yourself. I personally had no clue on how to invest in stocks, however, I invested in myself first by reading books, researching on the internet and watching YouTube videos on investing in stocks as well as attending seminars and workshops before I started investing in stocks. If I can do it, then everybody can also do it.

You can also speak to your bank or seek professional advice from independent stock brokers who can advise you on how to invest your savings or invest the money on your behalf. In addition, they can advise you on what to invest in at a fee.

The banks or independent brokers normally invest in high and medium risk shares and pay you certain percentage, they are likely to make more money because, they are expert in investing in shares. Warren Buffet calls these people Enterprise investors.

Apart from investing in shares, there are also other investment opportunities you can tap into, for example investing in Peer to Peer lending. These companies lend money to big companies and individuals, they normally give loans at a high interest to their debtors and make high returns for their investors. These are medium risk investment, because, if their debtors default in payment or are not able to pay the loan, then you are likely to lose your money. May I state that most investors receive their earnings on a monthly basis and get their investments back at the end of the loan term.

To reduce the impact of disappointments, it is always advisable to diversify your investment. You should not invest all your money in one set of Peer to Peer lenders, invest in two or three. The first and the most important thing to do is to research more on Peer to Peer lending and then invest in the ones that have existed for a long time and also pay decent profit per annum. Some of these companies have existed for years and therefore relatively safe to invest in them.

You can also invest in your pension. When you inform your employer to deduct a certain amount of money towards your pension, they might add some amount of money to it for you. Remember these are your life savings so you only have access to the money when you retire.

In the developing countries, especially in Africa, there are so many investment opportunities that yield substantial amount of interests. Again, the most important thing to do is to find a stable and democratic country to invest in. Most people in Africa invest in treasury bills, there is a 91-day treasury bill, 180-day treasury bill and one-year treasury bill.

When you invest in a 91-day treasury bill, the interest rate ranges between 10–15%, which means in a year you are likely to earn at least 10% profit. There are other investment opportunities such as fixed deposit, bonds, etc., however, treasury bills and fixed term deposits are the safest investment you can rely on.

According to Warren Buffet, it is advisable to diversify your portfolio and invest 25–50% of your money in stocks and 50–75% in bonds. This is because, when you invest in bonds you are assured of a specific percentage of profit every year, whereas in stocks, you will only earn depending on how the company performs.

If there is global crisis, uncertainty or instability, share prices could go down.

In Africa, you can open an account in any bank and invest in the treasury bills or fixed deposit, you can decide to re-invest the interest and allow the investment to earn you compound interest.

You are likely to earn interest between 20% to 25% on one-year fixed deposit. This means that it would take between four and five years to double any amount you invested.

Different banks offer different rates, for treasury bills it ranges from 10–15% per annum whereas one-year fixed deposit ranges from 20–25%. It is recommended to invest in a state-owned banks which pay decent rate than to invest in privately owned banks that pay higher interest rate. Even though the privately owned banks pay higher interest, the risk level in my view is higher than state-owned banks.

It is advisable to invest not more than 25% of your money in stocks or high-risk investment and invest 75% or more in bonds or safe and secure investment. It is also important to diversify your investment portfolios especially the high-risk investments so that if one fails you can fall on the others.

There are several platforms you can use to start investing in shares. You need to do your homework well to find the platforms that charge less commission or no commission at all. Most banks offer these services even though their charges are relatively high. The platforms that don't charge any interest when buying shares are recommended for beginners who don't have enough money to invest. You can invest as little as £50 without any commission because, some platforms charge commissions ranging from £5 per transaction to £15 commission per transaction.

Some of the platforms will give you more information than others; for example the financial report of companies and other relevant information that will help you make an informed decision are published on their platforms.

Earnings from stocks are taxable, it is therefore essential to seek professional advice from an accountant to help you prepare your accounts to ensure that you pay correct taxes. It is also advisable to invest in an ISA account through which your dividends could be paid into. You can decide to either re-invest your dividend or save it in the ISA account.

If you invest in the fee-paying platform, what you need to do is to save the money you want to invest and invest bigger amount each time and pay one fee instead of paying transaction fees on each small amount you invest.

Above all, it is advisable to invest in assets, most people including middle income earners who have become rich and also people who didn't inherit any wealth from their parents or family members and have become millionaires made it through investing in properties.

There are so many assets you can invest in, the most common ones are properties, gold, silver and gemstones. The property price in the UK and around the globe has been increasing every year, even if the price falls, it springs up again, but on the whole the property price increases so investors are guaranteed equity and passive income over time if the property is rented out. Most people invest in properties for long term benefit. This implies that they buy properties and rent them out for passive income, others invest in the properties for quick turn overs, so they buy the properties, renovate and sell them.

Other assets to invest in are gold and silver, these are called precious metals. The price of silver and gold historically have been increasing even though the price sometimes fluctuates. The fluctuations are good for investment, because, you buy when the price is low and sell when the price is high to make profits.

Investing in gemstones is another good investment opportunity as far as investing in assets are concerned. There are different types of gemstones you can invest in, these are: tanzanite, blue sapphire, diamond, ruby and emerald.

You can get tanzanite from China or Tanzania, blue sapphire from Sri Lanka or China, diamond from Ghana or South Africa, ruby from Nigeria or Zambia and emerald from Nigeria or Kenya. These gemstones could be purchased here in UK, keep for some time and sell when the price appreciates or buy from the countries where they are mined and sell in Europe or US.

If you want to invest in assets, then it is advisable to obey the 50/50% rule. This rule states that 'keep 50% of the assets you buy for long term gain and sell the remaining 50% for quick returns.'

This means that you hold on to 50% of the properties you would buy and sell the other 50%, only sell at the right time, that is when you have the opportunity to make profits.

Chapter 7

Investing in real estate

The easiest way of becoming rich is to invest in real state. So long as you work and have regular income, you stand a better chance of getting a mortgage and therefore building your real estate investment portfolio. All you need to do is to have a good credit record, this can be achieved by these three basic principles;

1. Having a regular income
2. Paying your bills on time and not defaulting in payment
3. Not having too many debts to pay

If you follow these three basic principles, you are likely to get a mortgage. Most banks or financial institutions will give you a loan to buy a property if they know you are capable of repaying this loan over a period of time. They normally spread the repayment over twenty-five years, so the younger you are, the lesser the amount of money you are likely to pay each month compared with an older person with similar circumstances, because, an older person would be required to pay the same amount of money in a shorter period of time. They take into consideration how long you have left to retire from work, they then calculate the total loan amount plus interest you will pay by the number of years left to your retirement.

Everybody will be expected to make an initial contribution towards the purchase of the property, this is called a deposit. Very few banks if any will give 100% mortgage without demanding a down payment towards the property. Most banks would demand between 5–10% deposit. Apart from the deposit, you may be required to pay stamp duty, which is normally 1% of the property. In UK, if you are buying a property for the first time, 'first time buyer' we call it, you will be exempted from paying stamp duty provided the price of the property is less than certain amount of money.

The government has introduced so many schemes to help people get onto the property ladder, especially if your income is low or haven't got enough money for the deposit so would be difficult to get a mortgage. One of such schemes is 'Help to Buy'. The government normally contributes 20% towards the deposit and the first time buyer contributes 5% adding up to 25%, this enables the buyer to buy a bigger property and still pay less per month. It is important to note that this money is not free, government will expect the money to be paid in five years without any interest, or pay interest after five years. The 20% loan amount given by government is also secured towards the property, so as the property value increases, government shares also increases. It is advisable to save money and pay off the money quickly because as the value of the property appreciates government shares will also appreciate.

If you can afford a two or three-bedroom property without 'Help to Buy', it is advisable to go for it instead of using 'Help to Buy' scheme, because, with the government 'Help to Buy', so long as the 20% hasn't been paid off, you cannot buy another property. If you have the intention of buying more properties any time soon after buying your first property, then research thoroughly on the government 'Help to Buy' scheme before committing to it. There are other schemes for example shared ownership, shared equity, etc, these are schemes run by property developers themselves, they let you own a percentage of the property and they also own the other percentage. You can buy off their shares of the property at any time. These are schemes you can use to buy a property to start your investment portfolio.

Different countries have different schemes, it is important to research more into all the available schemes and choose which will best suits you, book an appointment to talk to estate developers or visit their show rooms for up to date information so that as soon as you are ready to invest, you are likely to make the right choice. Alternatively, you can walk into your nearby estate agent office, they might give you useful advice at no cost.

Banks and financial institutions have their own criteria for giving loans. They always find out whether you can afford the loan or not, you might be eligible to get a particular loan amount which can secure a mortgage. However, financial institutions would take into consideration your outgoings including your other loans. They normally take your gross income and multiply it by 4.5 to check your affordability. If you have so many loans to pay, that would go against you. If you have been defaulting in bill payment, that will also go against you. Even if your credit report is not good, you can still get a loan but with a higher interest rate.

Interest rates on loans vary from lenders to lenders. It also depends on your credit report, people with good credit reports turn to have less interest rate, which means they would pay less interest on the loan amount they get from the banks.

Building your finances through planning as discussed earlier is necessary if you want to become rich.

It is essential you book an appointment with an estate agent and go for free assessment and affordability test, this will give you rough idea as to how much you can afford so that you can plan with it.

Once you have satisfied the three basic principles outlined above, you will then have to decide which property you want to go for. It is advisable to buy a three-bedroom property, the difference between a three bedroom and a two bedroom property is not that much. Purchase a three-bedroom house even if it outside the city centre. In UK for example, buying a property outside London is relatively cheaper, because, inner London properties are far more expensive than outer London properties. It is important you research extensively into the area you want to buy your property from once you know how much you can afford.

Buying a three-bedroom property is the best, because, you can rent out the other two rooms and live in one, the amount of money you will earn from the rent can either pay for half of the mortgage or pay all the utility bills. This means that you can save the utility bills and use it to invest or pay off your loans quicker. You should revise your personal budget once you buy your first property and plan to buy your second property within two years of buying your first property.

You could borrow money from the equity you have accrued on the property, add it to your personal savings and invest, this can be used as a deposit to buy another property.

The banks or financial institutions will give you another loan easily so long as you didn't default in your payment and can afford the deposit. The second property will attract a bigger deposit, it is normally between 20-25% in the UK. So long as you can afford the deposit, you need to go for another property. You should include in your plan to buy at least one house every two years. After buying five or more houses, you will be in a better position to invest bigger amount in shares, buy more assets and diversify your portfolio.

Once you have successfully acquired few properties, you could also look into investing in the developing countries. Alternatively, you can buy auction houses or dilapidated properties, renovate and rent them out. Once the properties have been renovated you can take equity from the properties for another investment or project. As soon as you get to this stage, you are on your way to become rich.

Friends and family as well as couples can put their resources together and use this real estate business model to acquire more properties for investment. They can earn more money from the equity on the property and use it to purchase their own houses.

There are also several websites which allow individuals to buy shares of property and earn rental income depending on their share value in that property. Such schemes also offer opportunities for people to invest every month to build their own property portfolios. It is expected that the property price will go up, so investors are likely to earn rental income every month and also benefit from the appreciation of the share price. It costs far less to invest in such properties compared to buying a house. People who are starting from a clean sheet and are building their credit or people who have been denied credit to own their own homes could invest in this kind of property so that they can sell off their shares to buy their own home once circumstances change for the better. Alternatively, you can team up with somebody with good credit record to purchase the property in their name. All they need to do is to put a charge on the property and have a proper legally bound agreement signed. With these, two or more people can raise at least £20,000 to buy a property.

It is advisable to start the real estate business by buying your own property if you can afford it. Buying your own house is like renting a house for free and investing the amount of money you would have used to rent the property towards your pension. If you carry on paying the mortgage without defaulting on the payment, in some years to come you will own the entire property. You can even decide to sell the property and cash in the money or sell it and use some of the money to buy a smaller property. On the other hand, when you rent a property, you would be contributing towards somebody's pension.

You can borrow money from the banks and use it to acquire more properties for other people to pay for these properties for you. This will enable you earn substantial amount of money to enter into the real estate business and even become real estate developer.

You can also invest in properties without going to the banks. You can approach Peer to Peer lenders once you find a property, their interest might be high, but if you can buy a house and afford the repayment why not use them? You can release equity after 6 months of purchase or slightly more to pay off the debt or pay off part of the debt. It is advisable to search more on Peer to Peer lending. They don't normally check your credit records and they are not as bureaucratic as the mainstream banks, however, they might secure their loan against the property by putting a charge on it.

Chapter 9

Bad debt and good debt

This subject is a controversial one and needs to be discussed in detail to ensure that everyone understands the differences and similarities between them. Debt can be defined as an amount of money owned or due. You can owe money by borrowing money from someone or from financial institution, you can also owe money when you buy goods and services on credit. Since money is a legal tenure, if you want to buy something but don't have enough money to buy it, you can borrow more money to top up what you have so that you can buy what you want.

Depending on what you borrow money for, the money you borrow could be categorised into one of the two main types of debts. The two main types of debts are good debt and bad debt. Good debt is a debt used to acquire an asset or assets that is capable of paying for the money owned and even earn you passive income whereas a bad debt is a debt that you owe that takes money from your pocket. Bad debt is capable of incurring more bad debts and could therefore lead you into financial difficulties.

Most people go for bad debt which has a potential damaging effect on their finances and eventually their future success. If bad debt is secured before getting your first job, as in the case of student loan, or if you secure bad debt at the start of your first employment, this could paralyse your future dream of becoming rich and lock you up in Group 2 as discussed in Chapter 3. Securing a bad debt seems good and exciting especially when the borrowed amount is used to secure your wants for luxury, but when it accumulates, it can cause serious financial problems for most people.

Financial institutions are there to make money for their investors, so they would be willing to loan money to people they know could pay for the loan with interest. They offer loans with an incredibly high interest rate to maximise their profits. You tend to pay between 20–40% interest without realising how much you have paid. This type of loan or debt would not only affect your future success and ability to invest but also cripple your chances of becoming rich.

Some of the bad debts are debts we incur when we use store cards or credit cards to purchase things we want. The interest rate on such cards is usually 29.9% per annum. This means that if you owe £1000, every year you would be paying almost £300 as interest. If you don't pay the amount you owe in full and decide to pay for the minimum amount of money you are expected to pay per month as stated on the monthly statement, you will be paying only the interest on the loan. This means that within four years you would have paid the financial institution £1000 as interest on the original amount you borrowed and still owe them the same £1000 you borrowed. This type of debt is referred to as bad debt and should be avoided at all cost.

Effective planning and budgeting as discussed in Chapter 1 is the best way of managing your finances. Most people take loans to buy a car, sometimes brand new car which depreciates in value the very moment you drive out of the showroom, such loan or debt is classified as bad debt, because, the repayment of the car loan will constantly take money from you and the car will depreciate in value over time. You will be paying a substantial amount of interest on the car loan. Some people buy a car or a van to run their business, i.e. to use the vehicle as taxi or cab or use it to transport goods and services. In other words if the vehicle is used for commercial purposes which brings in some income, then that loan or debt is not classified as bad debt, because, the car would be generating income to repay the loan and even earn you passive income with time.

In view of this, if you are buying a car for your personal use, it is advisable to save money over time using the 50/30/10/10% principle and ensure that you buy a car without paying any interest. Alternatively, you can save and make a bigger deposit to reduce the interest payment on the car. Car dealers always promote their business with different offers. If a car dealer offers 0% interest. This would be a good deal, however, you need to ask for more details, in other words find out what is written in the small print. There could be some terms and conditions you need to be aware of. Some of them could be 0% for the first year and 29.9% for the rest of the years.

Another bad debt is bank loans for holidays, to buy expensive clothes or to celebrate birthday party. It is good to celebrate and enjoy life as stated in my 50/30/10/10% principle, however, the money for such celebrations should come from your own savings. You could plan effectively and reduce the 50% or the other portions to increase your savings for celebrations and re-adjust your plan to accommodate circumstances if the need be, but to take a loan which has a potential damaging effect on your finances for things you want not things you need would not be recommended.

Good debt is a debt you take to invest which has the potential of earning you passive income. This debt could earn you substantial amount of money either in a long term or short term. Such debts repay itself and earn you extra income.

If you take a loan to buy a property, so long as you earn equity or passive income on the loan, it is classified as good debt. If you secure a loan of £100,000 from the bank which is spread over twenty-five years, when the property appreciates in value to about £200,000 in five years, you can decide to sell the property, pay interest of let's say £20,000 on the loan to the bank and still make a profit of about £80,000. However, if there is no equity on the property over the years and you tend to spend even more money on repairs, then the loan becomes a bad debt. In view of this scenario, some people classify securing a loan to own a house as bad debt until it begins to appreciate in value or earn you passive income. In my view, investing in a property whether as your private home or to rent it out is good debt because the value of the property will go up in the long term. If you buy a house to live in, you virtually pay 'rent' and own the house at some point. Even if the value of the house doesn't appreciate which is rarely the case, you still own a house so when you sell the property it can pay back the 'rent' you paid.

A good debt is when you secure a loan to buy a property which earns enough money to pay for the loan and even provide extra income as passive income. A good debt is also when you secure a loan from the bank to invest in shares or treasury bills which has the potential of earning enough to pay for the loan and earn extra income as well.

Securing a loan of £1000 from the bank with an interest of £200 for five years can earn you about £1000 if you invest it in fixed deposit in developing countries, for example Ghana. This investment would therefore earn you a net profit of about £800 in five years. In effect taking a loan to buy property or to invest in a fixed deposit to repay itself and earn passive income is a good debt.

If a bank offers you a loan and it could be used to buy a property to rent, go for it. Also, if the interest on the loan is very low and you know of any investment opportunity that could yield good returns compared with the interest rate on the loan, then it is a loan to go for, because, it is a good debt.

Avoid bad debt and embrace good debt if you want to be rich, in effect go into debt to become rich.

Chapter 10

Financial education

Becoming financially free or becoming rich depends on so many factors, the main factor is financial intelligence. If you are financially literate and aware of the steps you can follow to become rich, you will definitely make it so long as you obey the principles of money and follow the blueprints of becoming rich.

What is financial freedom? You become financially free when all your debts are paid off and your passive income become equal to or exceed your main source of income. At this stage, you are said to be financially free.

Financial education teaches you about the principles and concepts of money; how to plan, how to make money and how to invest money. It gives you all the secrets about money so that you know how to deal with money.

Financial education is the key to financial freedom, however, this is not taught in schools, so most people are not financially literate.

Most wrong financial decisions people make are because of lack of financial education. Our educational institutions don't teach how to plan your finances, how to make money, how to save, how to invest or how to manage your finances. This means that people have no choice than to learn from their mistakes. Even though there are so many books written about money, if you are not keen in investing or making money, you might not come across such books. Few people, normally city workers, businessmen and businesswomen tend to show an interest and participate in business seminars and workshops about business opportunities and how to invest.

The question is why are these seminars and workshops not organised for students at the secondary or tertiary level? Why are they organised at places where only few keen and business minded people have access to and can attend such life changing programs? Until financial education is introduced in our school curriculum, we need to educate ourselves and pass on the knowledge to our children to ensure that the next generation is financially literate. We need to be aware of the concept of money, how to manage and multiply money.

The parable of a rich man and the bags of gold in Matthew 25:14–30 can be used to describe the concept of money. According to the Bible, a rich man gave bags of gold to servants when travelling. To one he gave five bags of gold, to another two bags, and to another one bag, each according to his ability. Then he went on his journey. When he returned he called all of them for accountability. The one with five bags of gold had invested them and had increased them to ten bags of gold; the other servant with two bags of gold had also invested them and presented four bags of gold; to the third servant who had one bag of gold, presented the one that was given to him back to the master. The master was pleased with the two servants who invested their bags of gold. He was however, disappointed in the servant who did not invest in his bag of gold, so he took away the only one the servant was given and gave it to the one who had five bags of gold. The Bible also states in Matthew 25:29 that the rich shall be richer and the poor shall be poorer, this means that if you don't manage your money well, the little money you have shall be taken away from you and given to the rich. Below are extracts from the Bible, about the parable.

14 "Again, it will be like a man going on a journey, who called his servants and entrusted his wealth to them. 15 To one he gave five bags of gold, to another two bags, and to another one bag, each according to his ability. Then he went on his journey. 16 The man who had received five bags of gold went at once and put his money to work and gained five bags more. 17 So also, the one with two bags of gold gained two more. 18 But the man who had received one bag went off, dug a hole in the ground and hid his master's money. 19 "After a long time the master of those servants returned and settled accounts with them. 20 The man who had received five bags of gold brought the other five. 'Master,' he said, 'you entrusted me with five bags of gold. See, I have gained five more.' 21 "His master replied, 'Well done, good and faithful servant! You have been faithful with a few things; I will put you in charge of many things. Come and share your master's happiness!' 22 "The man with two bags of gold also came. 'Master,' he said, 'you entrusted me with two bags of gold; see, I have gained two more.' 23 "His master replied, 'Well done, good and faithful servant! You have been faithful with a few things; I will put you in charge of many things. Come and share your master's happiness!' 24 "Then the man who had received one bag of gold came. 'Master,' he said, 'I knew that you are a hard man, harvesting where you have not sown and gathering where you have not scattered seed. 25 So I was afraid and went out and hid your gold in the ground. See, here is what belongs to you.' 26 "His master replied, 'You wicked, lazy servant! So you knew that I harvest where I have not sown and gather where I have not scattered seed? 27 Well then, you should have put my money on deposit with the bankers, so that when I returned I would have received it back with interest. 28 "'So take the bag of gold from him and give it to the one who has ten bags. 29 For whoever has will be given more, and they will have an abundance. Whoever does not have, even what they have will be taken from them. 30 And throw that worthless servant outside, into the darkness, where there will be weeping and gnashing of teeth.' (Matthew 25:14–30).

What is happening in our world now is similar to the parables above. The big corporations, banks and financial institutions as well as the very rich people in our society have continued to increase their wealth and profit year in and year out, whereas most people continue to accumulate debts and become poorer and poorer.

Only few people who know how to manage their money well have been investing their money and earning substantial amounts. These people are making money on the daily basis increasing their wealth whereas majority of the people are struggling to cope financially. If you save and invest your money, you will earn more money just like the servant who was given five bags of gold, however, if you save the money without investing the money, you will earn virtually nothing on the money. This parable in the Bible clearly illustrates the concept of money and the importance of investment. If you want to be rich, you must save to invest, because, saving in the bank alone is like digging the soil and hiding your money. When you save in the bank, the banks use your money to trade or invest it and give you virtually nothing. It is important to know the difference between saving your money in the bank and investing your money in the bank. If you keep your money in your savings account or current account you will earn virtually nothing on it, however, when you invest in fixed deposit, bonds, shares, etc., in the bank you might earn some interest on it as discussed in the previous chapters.

Knowledge and understanding of the concept of money is crucial if you want to be financially free or become rich. The concept and principles of money clearly outline the blueprints of becoming rich. It is therefore necessary to know them. Money is like a seed, if you keep it safe or hide it in a box, it will remain there forever, however, if you plant it in the right environment under the right conditions needed for growth, it will grow, bear fruit and eventually multiply and produce more seeds. Each of the seeds will also grow under the right environmental conditions and multiply.

What environmental conditions do a seed need to be able to germinate, grow to become a tree and bear fruits? A seed needs the right environment which can provide the necessary nutrients to grow, this could be the soil or water in the case of hydroponics. In addition to the right environment, a seed needs three conditions to germinate. The first condition is water – which allows the seed to swell up to enable the embryo to start growing. The second condition needed is oxygen – this is used for respiration, transferring energy for germination. Warmth is the third condition, it speeds up the chemical reactions in the plant, speeding up the rate of germination.

This means that if any of these conditions is lacking, the germination or rate of germination would be affected. Money needs the right environment as well as environmental conditions to grow. It is up to the individual who has the money to do due diligence to find the right 'soil' or place to invest. The rate of growth of money can be enhanced or accelerated by the energy or drive to succeed. Money can grow or multiply if it is actively pursued, it should therefore be invested in one way or the other to provide the desired outcome. Hard work, the right attitude and self-discipline are necessary to provide the needed warmth for the 'reaction' or process of making more money to proceed. This means that laziness will affect the rate of growth of money, in effect it can adversely affect its growth.

If you plant a seed, water it and look after it properly, that seed will germinate, grow, bear more fruits or multiply to produce lots of seeds. However, if you don't look after it properly and leave it outside, birds might eat it or it might be washed away or destroyed. In effect you will miss the opportunity of multiplying this seed to give more seeds.

This scenario is comparable to money, because, if you have £500 and don't look after it properly or spend it wisely you will lose the money, also if you put this money in a money box, it will remain £500 for ever. It is likely to even lose its value, however, if you invest this money in the right place at the right time, this money could yield profit and multiply into lots of money. It is therefore essential to know how to gather these seeds (money), find the right environment and the right conditions necessary for growth, plant it, then sit back and watch this seed (money) grow. It is easy to lose all the money that come your way if you don't save to invest. The key to the concept of money is education.

According to Nelson Mandela, "Education is the most powerful weapon which you can use to change the world." To be able to reverse this trend so that we rather lend money to the banks and big companies, we need to improve our financial education. One way of improving it is by reading the *Financial Times* or financial newspapers and also watch business news such as Bloomberg to be aware of what is going on in the world market. Watching business news and improving your knowledge in financial education is necessary if you want to be rich. It is also essential to study about the stock market; you can research more on the internet, book online courses or watch YouTube videos on the stock market. You can achieve this by learning how to trade in stocks or how to invest as a beginner. All these will improve your financial education, this will enable you to save and invest to accumulate wealth.

Tom Corley, the author of *Rich Habits* studied 233 millionaires and found out that they have good habits which enable them to be successful. According to Corley, millionaires are savers – they save for the longest time, to accumulate wealth, in effect they accumulate the most wealth over a period of time. He also found out that millionaires are entrepreneurs – these are the people who take the least amount of time to accumulate most wealth. Which means that to be rich you need to educate yourself to be able to accumulate wealth over a short period of time and save for a long period of time. The question is how do you do this? All the ideas and strategies to make you rich are locked up somewhere especially in books, only a fraction of these ideas if any are still not tapped from peoples' brains. These ideas and strategies could be unlocked by reading extensively, you need to read books that can improve your knowledge and understanding of financial education. Read books for example, *Rich Habits* and *Poor Habits* by Tom Corley; *Financial Intelligence* by Benjamin Graham, *Rich Dad, Poor Dad* by Robert Kiyosaki , *Business Secrets from the Bible* by Rabbi

Daniel Lapin, books written by Dr Myles Munroe and many others. Watch the interviews of wealthy people like Richard Branson, Bill Gates, Warren Buffet, etc., and associate yourself with rich people, write to them or talk to them if you have the opportunity to meet them and ask them to mentor you. You can also study them or watch documentaries about them. All these will improve your knowledge and understanding about the rich people in our society and how to become one of them.

Improving your financial education will also increase your knowledge on how to start and run a successful business. Owning a business is one of the ways you can become rich. You can subscribe to online courses or enrol in a college to take part-time courses on how to start a business. There are so many career opportunities and government initiatives you can also tap into.

How can you impact the next generation? Having acquired this knowledge, it is essential to pass it on to the next generation since financial education is not taught in the mainstream schools and people get into financial difficulties before becoming financially literate.

Sometimes it might be too late to reverse the damage caused when you get into financial difficulties; it might also take longer to bounce back. Some people become depressed, others even commit suicide as a result of personal financial crisis. What you need to do is to use the weapon, i.e. financial education available to you to change this trend. Let's educate the next generation to be financially literate so that they can take the right decision for their future. According to Barack Obama, "All are equal, all are free, and all deserve a chance to pursue their full measure of happiness." All of us and the next generation deserve a chance to be financially free and enjoy life. Can we educate at least our children, relatives and our community about financial education?

YES, WE CAN!